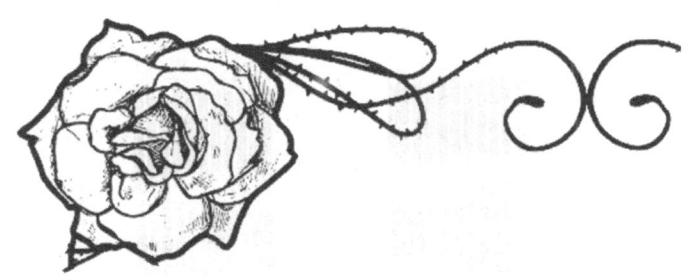

Journal For *Girl, Stop Apologizing*

A Shame-Free Plan For Embracing and Achieving Your Goals

By Rachel Hollis

BJ Richards

BONUS! FREE INSPIRATIONAL COLORING BOOK!

Get Yours Here: https://bjrichardsauthor.com/sccb-gsa-jn

Notification:

This is a journal designed to accompany the original work by Rachel Hollis, *Girl Stop Apologizing: A Shame-Free Plan For Embracing and Achieving Your Goals*. It is not meant to replace the original work.

This is an unofficial journal meant for educational and entertainment purposes only and has not been authorized, approved, licensed or endorsed by the original book's author or publisher and any of their licensees or affiliates.

Copyright and Disclaimer

Copyright © 2019, BJ Richards

All rights reserved. No part of this publication may be reproduced, distributed, or transmitted in any form or by any means, including photocopying, scanning, recording, or other electronic or mechanical methods, without the prior written permission of BJ Richards, except in the case of brief quotations embodied in critical reviews and certain other noncommercial uses permitted by copyright law.

Distribution of this book without the prior permission of BJ Richards is illegal, and therefore punishable by law. It is not legal to reproduce, duplicate or transmit any part of this document either in printed format or electronically. It is strictly prohibited to record this publication and storage of the document is not allowed without written permission from the BJ Richards. All rights reserved.

Disclaimer:

Legal Notice: - BJ Richards and the accompanying materials have used their best efforts in preparing the material. This book has been composed with the best intention of providing correct and reliable information. The information provided is offered solely for informational purposes and is universal as so. This information is presented without contract or any type of guarantee assurance.

This is an unofficial journal meant for educational and entertainment purposes only and has not been authorized, approved, licensed or endorsed by the original book's author or publisher and any of their licensees or affiliates.

BJ Richards makes no representation or warranties with respect to the accuracy, applicability, fitness or completeness of the contents of this book. The information contained in this book is strictly for educational purposes and entertainment purposes only. Therefore, if you wish to apply ideas contained in this book, you are taking full responsibility for your actions.

BJ Richards disclaims any warranties (express or implied), merchantability, or fitness for any particular purpose. BJ Richards shall in no event be held liable to any party for any direct, indirect, punitive, special, incidental or other consequential damages arising directly or indirectly from any use of this material, which is provided "as is", and without warranties.

Any and all trademarks, product names, logos, brands and other trademarks featured or referred to within this publication are owned by their respective trademark publications and owners themselves, are not affiliated with this book and are for clarifying purposes only.

BJ Richards does not warrant the performance, effectiveness or applicability of any sites listed or linked to in this book. All links are for information purposes only and are not warranted for content, accuracy or any other implied or explicit purpose.

indirect, punitive, special, incidental or other consequential damages arising directly or indirectly from any use of this material, which is provided "as is", and without warranties.

Any and all trademarks, product names, logos, brands and other trademarks featured or referred to within this publication are owned by their respective trademark publications and owners themselves, are not affiliated with this book and are for clarifying purposes only.

BJ Richards does not warrant the performance, effectiveness or applicability of any sites listed or linked to in this book. All links are for information purposes only and are not warranted for content, accuracy or any other implied or explicit purpose.

Recommended

I'm sure you already have this, but just in case, it is strongly recommended you purchase the original work by Ms. Hollis this journal is designed to compliment.

Girl, Stop Apologizing: A Shame-Free Plan for Embracing and Achieving Your Goals by Rachel Hollis

Get The Whole Set

The Perfect Workbook for This Program:

Many readers find it helpful to use a workbook to help them implement lessons and go deeper into the material that is presented.

I've created a workbook that is the perfect companion to the original work by Ms. Hollis, *Girl Stop Apologizing*. In my workbook you'll find worksheets and exercises designed to draw in your own life experiences so you can capitalize on what Ms. Hollis is presenting.

I think you'll love it!

Workbook Companion for Girl Stop Apologizing by Rachel Hollis: A Shame-Free Plan for Embracing and Achieving Your Goals by BJ Richards

The Perfect Planner for This Program:

You're going to need a place to set up, track and change your schedule on a weekly, monthly and yearly basis.

No problem... I have it covered for you! **My planner is designed specifically for the program presented by Ms. Hollis** in her original work, *Girl Stop Apologizing*. This will help you make your journey even easier!

Planner for Girl Stop Apologizing by Rachel Hollis: A Shame-Free Plan for Embracing and Achieving Your Goals by BJ Richards

You may also be interested in some of my other books:

1) Find out what coconut oil can really do for you without all the hype. Check out my best-selling book: *Coconut Oil Breakthrough: Boost Your Brain, Burn the Fat, Build Your Hair* by BJ Richards

Check it out here: https://www.amazon.com/Coconut-Oil-Breakthrough-Boost-Brain-ebook/dp/B01EGBA1FW/

2) Do you have a dog? Here's another best seller you may be interested in. You'll find out to deal with a number of issues safely and inexpensively at home. Find out all about it in my best-seller: *Coconut Oil and My Dog: Natural Pet Health for My Canine Friend* by BJ Richards

You can check it out here: https://www.amazon.com/Coconut-Oil-My-Dog-Natural-ebook/dp/B01MUF93U1/

3) Did you know apple cider vinegar and baking soda have some amazing health benefits? Plus, you can use them for so many things in the home and save a ton of money.

You'll find out all about it my boxset: *Apple Cider Vinegar and Baking Soda 101 for Beginners Box Set* by BJ Richards

Check it out here: https://www.amazon.com/Apple-Cider-Vinegar-Baking-Beginners-ebook/dp/B07DPCLWGB/

You can also go **my website** to find even more books I've written and some recommended by other authors: https://bjrichardsauthor.com

How To Use This Journal for Greater Personal Growth

Newbies welcome! My main goal for writing this journal was so anyone, even a complete newbie, can start to get immediate help in implementing the lessons Ms. Hollis has presented in her book: *Girl Stop Apologizing: A Shame-Free Plan for Embracing And Achieving Your Goals*.

This journal is meant as a companion to Ms. Hollis' original work. Studies have shown that journaling is an effective way to accelerate personal growth.

Each page includes a motivational quote you can use as an inspirational thought to help you keep your focus. These quotes have been life changing for thousands of people, helping them to move forward through life's challenges.

Plus, you'll find places to write out many of the activities Ms. Hollis suggests you do every day, such as:

- Track your daily habits.
- Write out 10 things you're grateful for that day.
- List your intention for the day.
- Reaffirm you goal and who you want to be.
- Take additional notes important to you.

This journal is easy to use with the right journal prompts you need to stay organized and on top of your personal goal.

You'll be able to track your progress and express yourself in just a matter of minutes!

Have fun, and enjoy the journey!

Date:

Daily Habits To Build

- [ ] Stayed Hydrated
- [ ] 30 Minutes Exercise
- [ ] 1 Junk Food Avoided
- [ ] Get Up 1 Hour Early
- [ ]

Intention For The Day:

Goal/Who I Want to Be:

10 Things I Am Grateful For Today / Notes:

"A goal is a dream with its workboots on." -- Rachel Hollis

Date:

Daily Habits To Build

- [ ] Stayed Hydrated
- [ ] 30 Minutes Exercise
- [ ] 1 Junk Food Avoided
- [ ] Get Up 1 Hour Early
- [ ]

Intention For The Day:

Goal/Who I Want to Be:

10 Things I Am Grateful For Today / Notes:

"To be a great champion you must believe you are the best. If you're not, pretend you are."   --Muhammad Ali

Date:

Daily Habits To Build

- [ ] Stayed Hydrated
- [ ] 30 Minutes Exercise
- [ ] 1 Junk Food Avoided
- [ ] Get Up 1 Hour Early
- [ ]

Intention For The Day:

Goal/Who I Want to Be:

10 Things I Am Grateful For Today / Notes:

"Someone else's opinion of you is none of your business."
— Rachel Hollis

Date:

Daily Habits To Build

- [ ] Stayed Hydrated
- [ ] 30 Minutes Exercise
- [ ] 1 Junk Food Avoided
- [ ] Get Up 1 Hour Early
- [ ]

Intention For The Day:

Goal/Who I Want to Be:

10 Things I Am Grateful For Today / Notes:

"We are what we repeatedly do. Excellence, therefore, is not an act, but a habit." -- Aristotle

Date:

Daily Habits To Build

- [ ] Stayed Hydrated
- [ ] 30 Minutes Exercise
- [ ] 1 Junk Food Avoided
- [ ] Get Up 1 Hour Early
- [ ]

Intention For The Day:

Goal/Who I Want to Be:

10 Things I Am Grateful For Today / Notes:

"Never break a promise to yourself." – Rachel Hollis

Date:

Daily Habits To Build

- [ ] Stayed Hydrated
- [ ] 30 Minutes Exercise
- [ ] 1 Junk Food Avoided
- [ ] Get Up 1 Hour Early
- [ ]

Intention For The Day:

Goal/Who I Want to Be:

10 Things I Am Grateful For Today / Notes:

"Dream big and dare to fail." – Norman Vaughan

Date:

Daily Habits To Build

- [ ] Stayed Hydrated
- [ ] 30 Minutes Exercise
- [ ] 1 Junk Food Avoided
- [ ] Get Up 1 Hour Early
- [ ]

Intention For The Day:

Goal/Who I Want to Be:

10 Things I Am Grateful For Today / Notes:

"You are beautiful and worthy of good things, and if you don't believe that, nobody will." – Rachel Hollis

Date:

Daily Habits To Build

- [ ] Stayed Hydrated
- [ ] 30 Minutes Exercise
- [ ] 1 Junk Food Avoided
- [ ] Get Up 1 Hour Early
- [ ]

Intention For The Day:

Goal/Who I Want to Be:

10 Things I Am Grateful For Today / Notes:

"With will one can do anything." – Samuel Smiles

Date:

Daily Habits To Build

- [ ] Stayed Hydrated
- [ ] 30 Minutes Exercise
- [ ] 1 Junk Food Avoided
- [ ] Get Up 1 Hour Early
- [ ]

Intention For The Day:

Goal/Who I Want to Be:

10 Things I Am Grateful For Today / Notes:

"Stop waiting on someone else to fix your life." – Rachel Hollis

Date:

Daily Habits To Build

- ☐ Stayed Hydrated
- ☐ 30 Minutes Exercise
- ☐ 1 Junk Food Avoided
- ☐ Get Up 1 Hour Early
- ☐

Intention For The Day:

Goal/Who I Want to Be:

10 Things I Am Grateful For Today / Notes:

"The only way of finding the limits of the possible is by going beyond them into the impossible." Arthur C Clark

Date:

Daily Habits To Build

- [ ] Stayed Hydrated
- [ ] 30 Minutes Exercise
- [ ] 1 Junk Food Avoided
- [ ] Get Up 1 Hour Early
- [ ]

Intention For The Day:

Goal/Who I Want to Be:

10 Things I Am Grateful For Today / Notes:

"If you're unhappy, that's on you." – Rachel Hollis

Date:

Daily Habits To Build

- ☐ Stayed Hydrated
- ☐ 30 Minutes Exercise
- ☐ 1 Junk Food Avoided
- ☐ Get Up 1 Hour Early
- ☐

Intention For The Day:

Goal/Who I Want to Be:

10 Things I Am Grateful For Today / Notes:

"Life consists not of holding good cards, but in playing the ones you hold well." —Josh Billings

Date:

Daily Habits To Build

- [ ] Stayed Hydrated
- [ ] 30 Minutes Exercise
- [ ] 1 Junk Food Avoided
- [ ] Get Up 1 Hour Early
- [ ]

Intention For The Day:

Goal/Who I Want to Be:

10 Things I Am Grateful For Today / Notes:

"The cost of your new life is your old one." – Rachel Hollis

Date:

Daily Habits To Build

- ☐ Stayed Hydrated
- ☐ 30 Minutes Exercise
- ☐ 1 Junk Food Avoided
- ☐ Get Up 1 Hour Early
- ☐

Intention For The Day:

Goal/Who I Want to Be:

10 Things I Am Grateful For Today / Notes:

"Do not wait till the iron is hot; but make it hot by striking." – William B. Sprague

Date:

Daily Habits To Build

- [ ] Stayed Hydrated
- [ ] 30 Minutes Exercise
- [ ] 1 Junk Food Avoided
- [ ] Get Up 1 Hour Early
- [ ]

Intention For The Day:

Goal/Who I Want to Be:

10 Things I Am Grateful For Today / Notes:

"Good news! Tomorrow is a new day." -- Rachel Hollis

Date:

Daily Habits To Build

- [ ] Stayed Hydrated
- [ ] 30 Minutes Exercise
- [ ] 1 Junk Food Avoided
- [ ] Get Up 1 Hour Early
- [ ]

Intention For The Day:

Goal/Who I Want to Be:

10 Things I Am Grateful For Today / Notes:

" Everyone has his burden. What counts is how you carry it." -- Merle Miller

Date:

Daily Habits To Build

- [ ] Stayed Hydrated
- [ ] 30 Minutes Exercise
- [ ] 1 Junk Food Avoided
- [ ] Get Up 1 Hour Early
- [ ]

Intention For The Day:

Goal/Who I Want to Be:

10 Things I Am Grateful For Today / Notes:

"Please, please, please stop letting your fear of getting it wrong to color every beautiful thing you're doing right." – Rachel Hollis

Date:

Daily Habits To Build

- [ ] Stayed Hydrated
- [ ] 30 Minutes Exercise
- [ ] 1 Junk Food Avoided
- [ ] Get Up 1 Hour Early
- [ ]

Intention For The Day:

Goal/Who I Want to Be:

10 Things I Am Grateful For Today / Notes:

"Nothing will ever be attempted if all possible objections must first be overcome." – Samuel Johnson

Date:

Daily Habits To Build

- [ ] Stayed Hydrated
- [ ] 30 Minutes Exercise
- [ ] 1 Junk Food Avoided
- [ ] Get Up 1 Hour Early
- [ ]

Intention For The Day:

Goal/Who I Want to Be:

10 Things I Am Grateful For Today / Notes:

"Work just as hard for pee-your-pants laughing moments as you do for all the other things." – Rachel Hollis

Date:

Daily Habits To Build

- ☐ Stayed Hydrated
- ☐ 30 Minutes Exercise
- ☐ 1 Junk Food Avoided
- ☐ Get Up 1 Hour Early
- ☐

Intention For The Day:

Goal/Who I Want to Be:

10 Things I Am Grateful For Today / Notes:

"Always look at what you have left. Never look at what you have lost." -- Robert H. Schuller

Date:

Daily Habits To Build

- [ ] Stayed Hydrated
- [ ] 30 Minutes Exercise
- [ ] 1 Junk Food Avoided
- [ ] Get Up 1 Hour Early
- [ ]

Intention For The Day:

Goal/Who I Want to Be:

10 Things I Am Grateful For Today / Notes:

"There isn't one right way to be a woman." – Rachel Hollis

Date:

Daily Habits To Build

- [ ] Stayed Hydrated
- [ ] 30 Minutes Exercise
- [ ] 1 Junk Food Avoided
- [ ] Get Up 1 Hour Early
- [ ]

Intention For The Day:

Goal/Who I Want to Be:

10 Things I Am Grateful For Today / Notes:

"Fortune favors the brave." – Publius Terrence

Date:

Daily Habits To Build

- [ ] Stayed Hydrated
- [ ] 30 Minutes Exercise
- [ ] 1 Junk Food Avoided
- [ ] Get Up 1 Hour Early
- [ ]

Intention For The Day:

Goal/Who I Want to Be:

10 Things I Am Grateful For Today / Notes:

"I believe it's not your weight that defines you." – Rachel Hollis

Date:

Daily Habits To Build

- [ ] Stayed Hydrated
- [ ] 30 Minutes Exercise
- [ ] 1 Junk Food Avoided
- [ ] Get Up 1 Hour Early
- [ ]

Intention For The Day:

Goal/Who I Want to Be:

10 Things I Am Grateful For Today / Notes:

"When the best of things are not possible, the best may be made of those that are." – Richard Hooker

Date:

Daily Habits To Build

- [ ] Stayed Hydrated
- [ ] 30 Minutes Exercise
- [ ] 1 Junk Food Avoided
- [ ] Get Up 1 Hour Early
- [ ]

Intention For The Day:

Goal/Who I Want to Be:

10 Things I Am Grateful For Today / Notes:

"The only person you need to be better than, is the one you were yesterday." – Rachel Hollis

Date:

Daily Habits To Build

- [ ] Stayed Hydrated
- [ ] 30 Minutes Exercise
- [ ] 1 Junk Food Avoided
- [ ] Get Up 1 Hour Early
- [ ]

Intention For The Day:

Goal / Who I Want to Be:

10 Things I Am Grateful For Today / Notes:

"Ability is what you're capable of doing. Motivation determines what you do. Attitude determines how well you do it." -- Lou Holtz

Date:

Daily Habits To Build

- [ ] Stayed Hydrated
- [ ] 30 Minutes Exercise
- [ ] 1 Junk Food Avoided
- [ ] Get Up 1 Hour Early
- [ ]

Intention For The Day:

Goal/Who I Want to Be:

10 Things I Am Grateful For Today / Notes:

"Slow down your yes." – Rachel Hollis

Date:

Daily Habits To Build

- [ ] Stayed Hydrated
- [ ] 30 Minutes Exercise
- [ ] 1 Junk Food Avoided
- [ ] Get Up 1 Hour Early
- [ ]

Intention For The Day:

Goal/Who I Want to Be:

10 Things I Am Grateful For Today / Notes:

"Amazing how we can light tomorrow with today." – Elizabeth Barrett Browning

Date:

Daily Habits To Build

- [ ] Stayed Hydrated
- [ ] 30 Minutes Exercise
- [ ] 1 Junk Food Avoided
- [ ] Get Up 1 Hour Early
- [ ]

Intention For The Day:

Goal/Who I Want to Be:

10 Things I Am Grateful For Today / Notes:

"This is the difference between living a life you always dreamed of or sitting alongside the death of the person you were meant to become." -- Rachel Hollis

Date:

Daily Habits To Build

- ☐ Stayed Hydrated
- ☐ 30 Minutes Exercise
- ☐ 1 Junk Food Avoided
- ☐ Get Up 1 Hour Early
- ☐

Intention For The Day:

Goal/Who I Want to Be:

10 Things I Am Grateful For Today / Notes:

"In every difficult situation is potential value. Believe this, then begin looking for it." – Norman Vincent Peale

Date:

Daily Habits To Build

- [ ] Stayed Hydrated
- [ ] 30 Minutes Exercise
- [ ] 1 Junk Food Avoided
- [ ] Get Up 1 Hour Early
- [ ]

Intention For The Day:

Goal/Who I Want to Be:

10 Things I Am Grateful For Today / Notes:

"You don't have to get it right all the time. You don't have to do things like anybody else's mom. You just have to care. Not only about them, but also about yourself." – Rachel Hollis

Date:

Daily Habits To Build

- [ ] Stayed Hydrated
- [ ] 30 Minutes Exercise
- [ ] 1 Junk Food Avoided
- [ ] Get Up 1 Hour Early
- [ ]

Intention For The Day:

Goal/Who I Want to Be:

10 Things I Am Grateful For Today / Notes:

"Believe with all your heart that you will do what you were made to do." – Orison Swett Marden

Date:

Daily Habits To Build

- [ ] Stayed Hydrated
- [ ] 30 Minutes Exercise
- [ ] 1 Junk Food Avoided
- [ ] Get Up 1 Hour Early
- [ ]

Intention For The Day:

Goal/Who I Want to Be:

10 Things I Am Grateful For Today / Notes:

"Spend more time feeding your spirit." – Rachel Hollis

Date:

Daily Habits To Build

- ☐ Stayed Hydrated
- ☐ 30 Minutes Exercise
- ☐ 1 Junk Food Avoided
- ☐ Get Up 1 Hour Early
- ☐

Intention For The Day:

Goal/Who I Want to Be:

10 Things I Am Grateful For Today / Notes:

"Knowing is not enough. We must apply. Willing is not enough, we must do." Johann Wolfgang von Goethe

Date:

Daily Habits To Build

- [ ] Stayed Hydrated
- [ ] 30 Minutes Exercise
- [ ] 1 Junk Food Avoided
- [ ] Get Up 1 Hour Early
- [ ]

Intention For The Day:

Goal/Who I Want to Be:

10 Things I Am Grateful For Today / Notes:

"No one cares about your dreams as much as you do." – **Rachel Hollis**

Date:

Daily Habits To Build

- [ ] Stayed Hydrated
- [ ] 30 Minutes Exercise
- [ ] 1 Junk Food Avoided
- [ ] Get Up 1 Hour Early
- [ ]

Intention For The Day:

Goal/Who I Want to Be:

10 Things I Am Grateful For Today / Notes:

"Nothing great was ever achieved without enthusiasm." – Ralph Waldo Emerson

Date:

Daily Habits To Build

- [ ] Stayed Hydrated
- [ ] 30 Minutes Exercise
- [ ] 1 Junk Food Avoided
- [ ] Get Up 1 Hour Early
- [ ]

Intention For The Day:

Goal/Who I Want to Be:

10 Things I Am Grateful For Today / Notes:

"Stop waiting for someday; someday is a myth." – Rachel Hollis

Date:

Daily Habits To Build

- ☐ Stayed Hydrated
- ☐ 30 Minutes Exercise
- ☐ 1 Junk Food Avoided
- ☐ Get Up 1 Hour Early
- ☐

Intention For The Day:

Goal/Who I Want to Be:

10 Things I Am Grateful For Today / Notes:

"I really concentrate on what's on my plate at the moment and do the very best I can." – Ruth Bader Ginsburg

Date:

Daily Habits To Build

- [ ] Stayed Hydrated
- [ ] 30 Minutes Exercise
- [ ] 1 Junk Food Avoided
- [ ] Get Up 1 Hour Early
- [ ]

Intention For The Day:

Goal/Who I Want to Be:

10 Things I Am Grateful For Today / Notes:

"...know this one great truth: you are in control of your own life." – Rachel Hollis

Date:

Daily Habits To Build

- [ ] Stayed Hydrated
- [ ] 30 Minutes Exercise
- [ ] 1 Junk Food Avoided
- [ ] Get Up 1 Hour Early
- [ ]

Intention For The Day:

Goal/Who I Want to Be:

10 Things I Am Grateful For Today / Notes:

"Real integrity is doing the right thing, knowing that nobody is going to know whether you did it or not." —Oprah

Date:

Daily Habits To Build

- [ ] Stayed Hydrated
- [ ] 30 Minutes Exercise
- [ ] 1 Junk Food Avoided
- [ ] Get Up 1 Hour Early
- [ ]

Intention For The Day:

Goal/Who I Want to Be:

10 Things I Am Grateful For Today / Notes:

"You are enough. Today. As you are." – Rachel Hollis

Date:

Daily Habits To Build

- ☐ Stayed Hydrated
- ☐ 30 Minutes Exercise
- ☐ 1 Junk Food Avoided
- ☐ Get Up 1 Hour Early
- ☐

Intention For The Day:

Goal/Who I Want to Be:

10 Things I Am Grateful For Today / Notes:

"The one way to get me to work my hardest was to doubt me." – Michelle Obama

Date:

Daily Habits To Build

- ☐ Stayed Hydrated
- ☐ 30 Minutes Exercise
- ☐ 1 Junk Food Avoided
- ☐ Get Up 1 Hour Early
- ☐

Intention For The Day:

Goal/Who I Want to Be:

10 Things I Am Grateful For Today / Notes:

"Not having the knowledge makes you teachable, not stupid." -- Rachel Hollis

Date:

Daily Habits To Build

- [ ] Stayed Hydrated
- [ ] 30 Minutes Exercise
- [ ] 1 Junk Food Avoided
- [ ] Get Up 1 Hour Early
- [ ]

Intention For The Day:

Goal/Who I Want to Be:

10 Things I Am Grateful For Today / Notes:

"Be a first-rate version of yourself, instead of a second-rate version of somebody else." – Judy Garland

Date:

Daily Habits To Build

- [ ] Stayed Hydrated
- [ ] 30 Minutes Exercise
- [ ] 1 Junk Food Avoided
- [ ] Get Up 1 Hour Early
- [ ]

Intention For The Day:

Goal/Who I Want to Be:

10 Things I Am Grateful For Today / Notes:

"Not being in shape makes you moldable, not lazy." – **Rachel Hollis**

Date:

Daily Habits To Build

- [ ] Stayed Hydrated
- [ ] 30 Minutes Exercise
- [ ] 1 Junk Food Avoided
- [ ] Get Up 1 Hour Early
- [ ]

Intention For The Day:

Goal/Who I Want to Be:

10 Things I Am Grateful For Today / Notes:

"Only do what your heart tells you." – Princess Diana

Date:

Daily Habits To Build

- [ ] Stayed Hydrated
- [ ] 30 Minutes Exercise
- [ ] 1 Junk Food Avoided
- [ ] Get Up 1 Hour Early
- [ ]

Intention For The Day:

Goal/Who I Want to Be:

10 Things I Am Grateful For Today / Notes:

"Not having the experience makes you eager, not ignorant." – Rachel Hollis

Date:

Daily Habits To Build

- ☐ Stayed Hydrated
- ☐ 30 Minutes Exercise
- ☐ 1 Junk Food Avoided
- ☐ Get Up 1 Hour Early
- ☐

Intention For The Day:

Goal/Who I Want to Be:

10 Things I Am Grateful For Today / Notes:

"We are all of us stars, and we deserve to twinkle." – Marilyn Monroe

Date:

Daily Habits To Build

- ☐ Stayed Hydrated
- ☐ 30 Minutes Exercise
- ☐ 1 Junk Food Avoided
- ☐ Get Up 1 Hour Early
- ☐

Intention For The Day:

Goal/Who I Want to Be:

10 Things I Am Grateful For Today / Notes:

> "OPO, other people's opinions. You down with it? Because if you are, you're giving all your power away." – Rachel Hollis

Date:

Daily Habits To Build

- [ ] Stayed Hydrated
- [ ] 30 Minutes Exercise
- [ ] 1 Junk Food Avoided
- [ ] Get Up 1 Hour Early
- [ ]

Intention For The Day:

Goal/Who I Want to Be:

10 Things I Am Grateful For Today / Notes:

"Nothing is impossible. The word itself says 'I'm possible!'" -- Audrey Hepburn

Date:

Daily Habits To Build

- [ ] Stayed Hydrated
- [ ] 30 Minutes Exercise
- [ ] 1 Junk Food Avoided
- [ ] Get Up 1 Hour Early
- [ ]

Intention For The Day:

Goal/Who I Want to Be:

10 Things I Am Grateful For Today / Notes:

"You guys, mommy guilt is bull____!." – Rachel Hollis

Date:

Daily Habits To Build

- [ ] Stayed Hydrated
- [ ] 30 Minutes Exercise
- [ ] 1 Junk Food Avoided
- [ ] Get Up 1 Hour Early
- [ ]

Intention For The Day:

Goal/Who I Want to Be:

10 Things I Am Grateful For Today / Notes:

"Remember, no one can make you feel inferior without your consent." – Eleanor Roosevelt

Date:

Daily Habits To Build

- [ ] Stayed Hydrated
- [ ] 30 Minutes Exercise
- [ ] 1 Junk Food Avoided
- [ ] Get Up 1 Hour Early
- [ ]

Intention For The Day:

Goal/Who I Want to Be:

10 Things I Am Grateful For Today / Notes:

"Girl, maybe you should get it tattooed on your body, but it's this simple: Go All In" – Rachel Hollis

Date:

Daily Habits To Build

- ☐ Stayed Hydrated
- ☐ 30 Minutes Exercise
- ☐ 1 Junk Food Avoided
- ☐ Get Up 1 Hour Early
- ☐

Intention For The Day:

Goal/Who I Want to Be:

10 Things I Am Grateful For Today / Notes:

"I am not afraid of storms, for I am learning how to sail my ship." – Louisa May Alcott

Date:

Daily Habits To Build

- [ ] Stayed Hydrated
- [ ] 30 Minutes Exercise
- [ ] 1 Junk Food Avoided
- [ ] Get Up 1 Hour Early
- [ ]

Intention For The Day:

Goal/Who I Want to Be:

10 Things I Am Grateful For Today / Notes:

"Who you are is defined by the next decision you make, not the last one." – Rachel Hollis

Date:

Daily Habits To Build

- [ ] Stayed Hydrated
- [ ] 30 Minutes Exercise
- [ ] 1 Junk Food Avoided
- [ ] Get Up 1 Hour Early
- [ ]

Intention For The Day:

Goal/Who I Want to Be:

10 Things I Am Grateful For Today / Notes:

"The final forming of one's character lies in their own hands." – Anne Frank

Date:

Daily Habits To Build

- [ ] Stayed Hydrated
- [ ] 30 Minutes Exercise
- [ ] 1 Junk Food Avoided
- [ ] Get Up 1 Hour Early
- [ ]

Intention For The Day:

Goal/Who I Want to Be:

10 Things I Am Grateful For Today / Notes:

"There is so much untapped potential inside of people who are too afraid to give themselves a chance." -- Rachel Hollis

Date:

Daily Habits To Build

- [ ] Stayed Hydrated
- [ ] 30 Minutes Exercise
- [ ] 1 Junk Food Avoided
- [ ] Get Up 1 Hour Early
- [ ]

Intention For The Day:

Goal/Who I Want to Be:

10 Things I Am Grateful For Today / Notes:

"I alone cannot change the world, but I can cast a stone across the waters to create many ripples." – Mother Teresa

Date:

Daily Habits To Build

- [ ] Stayed Hydrated
- [ ] 30 Minutes Exercise
- [ ] 1 Junk Food Avoided
- [ ] Get Up 1 Hour Early
- [ ]

Intention For The Day:

Goal / Who I Want to Be:

10 Things I Am Grateful For Today / Notes:

"Maybe the hardest part of life is just having the courage to try." – Rachel Hollis

Date:

Daily Habits To Build

- ☐ Stayed Hydrated
- ☐ 30 Minutes Exercise
- ☐ 1 Junk Food Avoided
- ☐ Get Up 1 Hour Early
- ☐

Intention For The Day:

Goal/Who I Want to Be:

10 Things I Am Grateful For Today / Notes:

"If your actions create a legacy that inspires others to dream more, learn more, do more and become more, then you are an excellent leader." – Dolly Parton

Date:

Daily Habits To Build

- [ ] Stayed Hydrated
- [ ] 30 Minutes Exercise
- [ ] 1 Junk Food Avoided
- [ ] Get Up 1 Hour Early
- [ ]

Intention For The Day:

Goal/Who I Want to Be:

10 Things I Am Grateful For Today / Notes:

"Our words have power, but our actions shape our lives." – Rachel Hollis

Date:

Daily Habits To Build

- ☐ Stayed Hydrated
- ☐ 30 Minutes Exercise
- ☐ 1 Junk Food Avoided
- ☐ Get Up 1 Hour Early
- ☐

Intention For The Day:

Goal/Who I Want to Be:

10 Things I Am Grateful For Today / Notes:

"Just don't give up trying to do what you really want to do. Where there is love and inspiration, I don't think you can go wrong." – Ella Fitzgerald

Date:

Daily Habits To Build

- [ ] Stayed Hydrated
- [ ] 30 Minutes Exercise
- [ ] 1 Junk Food Avoided
- [ ] Get Up 1 Hour Early
- [ ]

Intention For The Day:

Goal/Who I Want to Be:

10 Things I Am Grateful For Today / Notes:

"People treat you with as much, or as little respect as you allow them to." – Rachel Hollis

Date:

Daily Habits To Build

- ☐ Stayed Hydrated
- ☐ 30 Minutes Exercise
- ☐ 1 Junk Food Avoided
- ☐ Get Up 1 Hour Early
- ☐

Intention For The Day:

Goal/Who I Want to Be:

10 Things I Am Grateful For Today / Notes:

"How wonderful it is that no one need wait a single moment before starting to improve the world." – Anne Frank

Date:

Daily Habits To Build

- [ ] Stayed Hydrated
- [ ] 30 Minutes Exercise
- [ ] 1 Junk Food Avoided
- [ ] Get Up 1 Hour Early
- [ ]

Intention For The Day:

Goal / Who I Want to Be:

10 Things I Am Grateful For Today / Notes:

"Friends, it's not about the goal or the dream you have. It's about who you become on your way to that goal." – Rachel Hollis

Date:

Daily Habits To Build

- ☐ Stayed Hydrated
- ☐ 30 Minutes Exercise
- ☐ 1 Junk Food Avoided
- ☐ Get Up 1 Hour Early
- ☐

Intention For The Day:

Goal/Who I Want to Be:

10 Things I Am Grateful For Today / Notes:

"You really have to love yourself to get anything done in this world." -- Lucile Ball

Date:

Daily Habits To Build

- [ ] Stayed Hydrated
- [ ] 30 Minutes Exercise
- [ ] 1 Junk Food Avoided
- [ ] Get Up 1 Hour Early
- [ ]

Intention For The Day:

Goal/Who I Want to Be:

10 Things I Am Grateful For Today / Notes:

"When you really want something, you will find a way. When you don't really want something, you'll find an excuse." – Rachel Hollis

Date:

Daily Habits To Build

- [ ] Stayed Hydrated
- [ ] 30 Minutes Exercise
- [ ] 1 Junk Food Avoided
- [ ] Get Up 1 Hour Early
- [ ]

Intention For The Day:

Goal/Who I Want to Be:

10 Things I Am Grateful For Today / Notes:

"And if you can't go straight ahead, you go around the corner." -- Cher

Date:

Daily Habits To Build

- [ ] Stayed Hydrated
- [ ] 30 Minutes Exercise
- [ ] 1 Junk Food Avoided
- [ ] Get Up 1 Hour Early
- [ ]

Intention For The Day:

Goal/Who I Want to Be:

10 Things I Am Grateful For Today / Notes:

"Your dream is worth fighting for, and while you're not in control of what life throws at you, you are in control of the fight." – Rachel Hollis

Date:

Daily Habits To Build

- ☐ Stayed Hydrated
- ☐ 30 Minutes Exercise
- ☐ 1 Junk Food Avoided
- ☐ Get Up 1 Hour Early
- ☐

Intention For The Day:

Goal/Who I Want to Be:

10 Things I Am Grateful For Today / Notes:

"I avoid looking back. I prefer good memories to regrets."
— Grace Kelly

Date:

Daily Habits To Build

- [ ] Stayed Hydrated
- [ ] 30 Minutes Exercise
- [ ] 1 Junk Food Avoided
- [ ] Get Up 1 Hour Early
- [ ]

Intention For The Day:

Goal/Who I Want to Be:

10 Things I Am Grateful For Today / Notes:

"You must choose to be happy, grateful, and fulfilled. If you make that choice every single day, regardless of where you are or what's happening, you will be happy." -- Rachel Hollis

Date:

Daily Habits To Build

- [ ] Stayed Hydrated
- [ ] 30 Minutes Exercise
- [ ] 1 Junk Food Avoided
- [ ] Get Up 1 Hour Early
- [ ]

Intention For The Day:

Goal/Who I Want to Be:

10 Things I Am Grateful For Today / Notes:

"The most difficult thing is the decision to act, the rest is merely tenacity." – Amelia Earhart

Date:

Daily Habits To Build

- [ ] Stayed Hydrated
- [ ] 30 Minutes Exercise
- [ ] 1 Junk Food Avoided
- [ ] Get Up 1 Hour Early
- [ ]

Intention For The Day:

Goal/Who I Want to Be:

10 Things I Am Grateful For Today / Notes:

"Decide that you care more about creating your magic and pushing it out into the world than you do about how it will be received." – *Rachel Hollis*

Date:

Daily Habits To Build

- [ ] Stayed Hydrated
- [ ] 30 Minutes Exercise
- [ ] 1 Junk Food Avoided
- [ ] Get Up 1 Hour Early
- [ ]

Intention For The Day:

Goal/Who I Want to Be:

10 Things I Am Grateful For Today / Notes:

"It's never too late. Never too late to change your life, never too late to be happy." — Jane Fonda

Date:

Daily Habits To Build

- [ ] Stayed Hydrated
- [ ] 30 Minutes Exercise
- [ ] 1 Junk Food Avoided
- [ ] Get Up 1 Hour Early
- [ ]

Intention For The Day:

Goal/Who I Want to Be:

10 Things I Am Grateful For Today / Notes:

"The only thing worse than giving up, is wishing that you hadn't." – Rachel Hollis

Date:

Daily Habits To Build

- ☐ Stayed Hydrated
- ☐ 30 Minutes Exercise
- ☐ 1 Junk Food Avoided
- ☐ Get Up 1 Hour Early
- ☐

Intention For The Day:

Goal/Who I Want to Be:

10 Things I Am Grateful For Today / Notes:

"You only live once. But if you do it right, once is enough." – Mae West

Date:

Daily Habits To Build

- [ ] Stayed Hydrated
- [ ] 30 Minutes Exercise
- [ ] 1 Junk Food Avoided
- [ ] Get Up 1 Hour Early
- [ ]

Intention For The Day:

Goal / Who I Want to Be:

10 Things I Am Grateful For Today / Notes:

"You must choose to be happy, grateful, and fulfilled. If you make that choice every single day, regardless of where you are or what's happening, you will be happy." – Rachel Hollis

Date:

Daily Habits To Build

- [ ] Stayed Hydrated
- [ ] 30 Minutes Exercise
- [ ] 1 Junk Food Avoided
- [ ] Get Up 1 Hour Early
- [ ]

Intention For The Day:

Goal/Who I Want to Be:

10 Things I Am Grateful For Today / Notes:

"Champions keep playing until they get it right."
— Billie Jean King

Date:

Daily Habits To Build

- [ ] Stayed Hydrated
- [ ] 30 Minutes Exercise
- [ ] 1 Junk Food Avoided
- [ ] Get Up 1 Hour Early
- [ ]

Intention For The Day:

Goal/Who I Want to Be:

10 Things I Am Grateful For Today / Notes:

"Your life is supposed to be a journey from one unique place to another; it's not supposed to be a merry-go-round that brings you back to the same spot over and over again." – Rachel Hollis

Date:

Daily Habits To Build

- ☐ Stayed Hydrated
- ☐ 30 Minutes Exercise
- ☐ 1 Junk Food Avoided
- ☐ Get Up 1 Hour Early
- ☐

Intention For The Day:

Goal/Who I Want to Be:

10 Things I Am Grateful For Today / Notes:

"You become what you believe." -- Oprah

Date:

Daily Habits To Build

- [ ] Stayed Hydrated
- [ ] 30 Minutes Exercise
- [ ] 1 Junk Food Avoided
- [ ] Get Up 1 Hour Early
- [ ]

Intention For The Day:

Goal/Who I Want to Be:

10 Things I Am Grateful For Today / Notes:

"You were not made to be small. You are not a little girl. You are a grown woman, and it's time you grew up." –
Rachel Hollis

Date:

Daily Habits To Build

- [ ] Stayed Hydrated
- [ ] 30 Minutes Exercise
- [ ] 1 Junk Food Avoided
- [ ] Get Up 1 Hour Early
- [ ]

Intention For The Day:

Goal/Who I Want to Be:

10 Things I Am Grateful For Today / Notes:

"When you have a dream, you've got to grab it and never let it go." – Carol Burnett

Date:

Daily Habits To Build

- ☐ Stayed Hydrated
- ☐ 30 Minutes Exercise
- ☐ 1 Junk Food Avoided
- ☐ Get Up 1 Hour Early
- ☐

Intention For The Day:

Goal/Who I Want to Be:

10 Things I Am Grateful For Today / Notes:

"Our society makes plenty of room for complacency or laziness; we're rarely surrounded by accountability." – Rachel Hollis

Date:

Daily Habits To Build

- ☐ Stayed Hydrated
- ☐ 30 Minutes Exercise
- ☐ 1 Junk Food Avoided
- ☐ Get Up 1 Hour Early
- ☐

Intention For The Day:

Goal/Who I Want to Be:

10 Things I Am Grateful For Today / Notes:

"It takes a great deal of courage to stand up to your enemies, but even more to stand up to your friends." – JK Rowling

Date:

Daily Habits To Build

- [ ] Stayed Hydrated
- [ ] 30 Minutes Exercise
- [ ] 1 Junk Food Avoided
- [ ] Get Up 1 Hour Early
- [ ]

Intention For The Day:

Goal/Who I Want to Be:

10 Things I Am Grateful For Today / Notes:

"If time has taught me anything, it's that our differences are what make this life unique." -- Rachel Hollis

Date:

Daily Habits To Build

- [ ] Stayed Hydrated
- [ ] 30 Minutes Exercise
- [ ] 1 Junk Food Avoided
- [ ] Get Up 1 Hour Early
- [ ]

Intention For The Day:

Goal/Who I Want to Be:

10 Things I Am Grateful For Today / Notes:

"Dreaming, after all, is a form of planning." – Gloria Steinem

Date:

Daily Habits To Build

- ☐ Stayed Hydrated
- ☐ 30 Minutes Exercise
- ☐ 1 Junk Food Avoided
- ☐ Get Up 1 Hour Early
- ☐

Intention For The Day:

Goal/Who I Want to Be:

10 Things I Am Grateful For Today / Notes:

"Your integrity is the only thing they can't take away from you." – Rachel Hollis

Date:

Daily Habits To Build

- [ ] Stayed Hydrated
- [ ] 30 Minutes Exercise
- [ ] 1 Junk Food Avoided
- [ ] Get Up 1 Hour Early
- [ ]

Intention For The Day:

Goal/Who I Want to Be:

10 Things I Am Grateful For Today / Notes:

"The most common way people give up their power is by thinking they don't have any." – Alice Walker

Date:

Daily Habits To Build

- [ ] Stayed Hydrated
- [ ] 30 Minutes Exercise
- [ ] 1 Junk Food Avoided
- [ ] Get Up 1 Hour Early
- [ ]

Intention For The Day:

Goal/Who I Want to Be:

10 Things I Am Grateful For Today / Notes:

"You need to get up off the sofa or out of the bed and move around. Get out of the fog that you have been living in and see your life for what it is." — Rachel Hollis

Date:

Daily Habits To Build

- ☐ Stayed Hydrated
- ☐ 30 Minutes Exercise
- ☐ 1 Junk Food Avoided
- ☐ Get Up 1 Hour Early
- ☐

Intention For The Day:

Goal/Who I Want to Be:

10 Things I Am Grateful For Today / Notes:

"If you know you're going to fail, then fail gloriously." – Cate Blanchett

Date:

Daily Habits To Build

- [ ] Stayed Hydrated
- [ ] 30 Minutes Exercise
- [ ] 1 Junk Food Avoided
- [ ] Get Up 1 Hour Early
- [ ]

Intention For The Day:

Goal/Who I Want to Be:

10 Things I Am Grateful For Today / Notes:

"Nothing that lasts is accomplished quickly." – **Rachel Hollis**

Date:

Daily Habits To Build

- ☐ Stayed Hydrated
- ☐ 30 Minutes Exercise
- ☐ 1 Junk Food Avoided
- ☐ Get Up 1 Hour Early
- ☐

Intention For The Day:

Goal/Who I Want to Be:

10 Things I Am Grateful For Today / Notes:

"Without an open-minded mind, you can never be a great success." – Martha Stewart

Date:

Daily Habits To Build

- [ ] Stayed Hydrated
- [ ] 30 Minutes Exercise
- [ ] 1 Junk Food Avoided
- [ ] Get Up 1 Hour Early
- [ ]

Intention For The Day:

Goal / Who I Want to Be:

10 Things I Am Grateful For Today / Notes:

"Girl, get ahold of your life. Stop medicating, stop hiding out, stop being afraid, stop giving away pieces of yourself, stop saying you can't do it." – Rachel Hollis

Date:

Daily Habits To Build

- [ ] Stayed Hydrated
- [ ] 30 Minutes Exercise
- [ ] 1 Junk Food Avoided
- [ ] Get Up 1 Hour Early
- [ ]

Intention For The Day:

Goal/Who I Want to Be:

10 Things I Am Grateful For Today / Notes:

"Fearlessness is not the absence of fear. It's the mastery of fear. It's about getting up one more time than we fall down." – Arianna Huffington

Date:

Daily Habits To Build

- [ ] Stayed Hydrated
- [ ] 30 Minutes Exercise
- [ ] 1 Junk Food Avoided
- [ ] Get Up 1 Hour Early
- [ ]

Intention For The Day:

Goal/Who I Want to Be:

10 Things I Am Grateful For Today / Notes:

"Get up, right now. Rise up from where you've been, scrub away the tears and the pain of yesterday, and start again... Girl wash your face!" – Rachel Hollis

Date:

Daily Habits To Build

- [ ] Stayed Hydrated
- [ ] 30 Minutes Exercise
- [ ] 1 Junk Food Avoided
- [ ] Get Up 1 Hour Early
- [ ]

Intention For The Day:

Goal/Who I Want to Be:

10 Things I Am Grateful For Today / Notes:

"Take criticism seriously, but not personally. If there is truth or merit in the criticism, try to learn from it. Otherwise, let it roll right off you." – Hillary Clinton

Date:

Daily Habits To Build

- [ ] Stayed Hydrated
- [ ] 30 Minutes Exercise
- [ ] 1 Junk Food Avoided
- [ ] Get Up 1 Hour Early
- [ ]

Intention For The Day:

Goal/Who I Want to Be:

10 Things I Am Grateful For Today / Notes:

"The word no is not a reason to top. Instead, think of it as a detour or a yield sign. No means merge with caution." – Rachel Hollis

Date:

Daily Habits To Build

- [ ] Stayed Hydrated
- [ ] 30 Minutes Exercise
- [ ] 1 Junk Food Avoided
- [ ] Get Up 1 Hour Early
- [ ]

Intention For The Day:

Goal/Who I Want to Be:

10 Things I Am Grateful For Today / Notes:

"You may have to fight a battle more than once to win it." – Margaret Thatcher

Date:

Daily Habits To Build

- [ ] Stayed Hydrated
- [ ] 30 Minutes Exercise
- [ ] 1 Junk Food Avoided
- [ ] Get Up 1 Hour Early
- [ ]

Intention For The Day:

Goal/Who I Want to Be:

10 Things I Am Grateful For Today / Notes:

"The truth? You, and only you, are ultimately responsible for who you become and how happy you are." -- Rachel Hollis

Date:

Daily Habits To Build

- [ ] Stayed Hydrated
- [ ] 30 Minutes Exercise
- [ ] 1 Junk Food Avoided
- [ ] Get Up 1 Hour Early
- [ ]

Intention For The Day:

Goal/Who I Want to Be:

10 Things I Am Grateful For Today / Notes:

" Don't compromise yourself. You are all you've got." – Janice Joplin

Date:

Daily Habits To Build

- [ ] Stayed Hydrated
- [ ] 30 Minutes Exercise
- [ ] 1 Junk Food Avoided
- [ ] Get Up 1 Hour Early
- [ ]

Intention For The Day:

Goal/Who I Want to Be:

10 Things I Am Grateful For Today / Notes:

"I recognized a great truth: if I wanted a better life than the one I'd been born into, it was up to me to create it." – Rachel Hollis

Date:

Daily Habits To Build

- [ ] Stayed Hydrated
- [ ] 30 Minutes Exercise
- [ ] 1 Junk Food Avoided
- [ ] Get Up 1 Hour Early
- [ ]

Intention For The Day:

Goal/Who I Want to Be:

10 Things I Am Grateful For Today / Notes:

"The future belongs to those who believe in the beauty of their dreams." – Eleanor Roosevelt

Date:

Daily Habits To Build

- [ ] Stayed Hydrated
- [ ] 30 Minutes Exercise
- [ ] 1 Junk Food Avoided
- [ ] Get Up 1 Hour Early
- [ ]

Intention For The Day:

Goal/Who I Want to Be:

10 Things I Am Grateful For Today / Notes:

"I am successful because I never once believed my dreams were someone else's to manage." – Rachel Hollis

Date:

Daily Habits To Build

- [ ] Stayed Hydrated
- [ ] 30 Minutes Exercise
- [ ] 1 Junk Food Avoided
- [ ] Get Up 1 Hour Early
- [ ]

Intention For The Day:

Goal/Who I Want to Be:

10 Things I Am Grateful For Today / Notes:

"If people are doubting how far you can go, go so far you can't hear them anymore." – Michele Ruiz

Date:

Daily Habits To Build

- [ ] Stayed Hydrated
- [ ] 30 Minutes Exercise
- [ ] 1 Junk Food Avoided
- [ ] Get Up 1 Hour Early
- [ ]

Intention For The Day:

Goal/Who I Want to Be:

10 Things I Am Grateful For Today / Notes:

"You are allowed to want more for yourself for no other reason than because it makes your heart happy." – Rachel Hollis

Date:

Daily Habits To Build

- [ ] Stayed Hydrated
- [ ] 30 Minutes Exercise
- [ ] 1 Junk Food Avoided
- [ ] Get Up 1 Hour Early
- [ ]

Intention For The Day:

Goal/Who I Want to Be:

10 Things I Am Grateful For Today / Notes:

"Don't follow the crowd. Let the crowd follow you." – Margaret Thatcher

Date:

Daily Habits To Build

- ☐ Stayed Hydrated
- ☐ 30 Minutes Exercise
- ☐ 1 Junk Food Avoided
- ☐ Get Up 1 Hour Early
- ☐

Intention For The Day:

Goal/Who I Want to Be:

10 Things I Am Grateful For Today / Notes:

"Embracing chaos might be the journey we take to finding peace." – Rachel Hollis

Date:

Daily Habits To Build

- [ ] Stayed Hydrated
- [ ] 30 Minutes Exercise
- [ ] 1 Junk Food Avoided
- [ ] Get Up 1 Hour Early
- [ ]

Intention For The Day:

Goal/Who I Want to Be:

10 Things I Am Grateful For Today / Notes:

"The most important power we have is within ourselves."
– Cate Blanchett

Date:

Daily Habits To Build

- [ ] Stayed Hydrated
- [ ] 30 Minutes Exercise
- [ ] 1 Junk Food Avoided
- [ ] Get Up 1 Hour Early
- [ ]

Intention For The Day:

Goal/Who I Want to Be:

10 Things I Am Grateful For Today / Notes:

"I cannot continue to live as half myself simply because it's hard for others to handle all of me." – Rachel Hollis

Date:

Daily Habits To Build

- [ ] Stayed Hydrated
- [ ] 30 Minutes Exercise
- [ ] 1 Junk Food Avoided
- [ ] Get Up 1 Hour Early
- [ ]

Intention For The Day:

Goal / Who I Want to Be:

10 Things I Am Grateful For Today / Notes:

"You must do the things you think you cannot do." – Eleanor Roosevelt

Date:

Daily Habits To Build

- [ ] Stayed Hydrated
- [ ] 30 Minutes Exercise
- [ ] 1 Junk Food Avoided
- [ ] Get Up 1 Hour Early
- [ ]

Intention For The Day:

Goal/Who I Want to Be:

10 Things I Am Grateful For Today / Notes:

"Ambition is not a dirty word." – Rachel Hollis

Date:

Daily Habits To Build

- [ ] Stayed Hydrated
- [ ] 30 Minutes Exercise
- [ ] 1 Junk Food Avoided
- [ ] Get Up 1 Hour Early
- [ ]

Intention For The Day:

Goal/Who I Want to Be:

10 Things I Am Grateful For Today / Notes:

"Think like a queen. A queen is not afraid to fail. Failure is another stepping stone to greatness." – Oprah

Date:

Daily Habits To Build

- [ ] Stayed Hydrated
- [ ] 30 Minutes Exercise
- [ ] 1 Junk Food Avoided
- [ ] Get Up 1 Hour Early
- [ ]

Intention For The Day:

Goal / Who I Want to Be:

10 Things I Am Grateful For Today / Notes:

"You are more than you have become." – Rachel Hollis

Date:

Daily Habits To Build

- [ ] Stayed Hydrated
- [ ] 30 Minutes Exercise
- [ ] 1 Junk Food Avoided
- [ ] Get Up 1 Hour Early
- [ ]

Intention For The Day:

Goal/Who I Want to Be:

10 Things I Am Grateful For Today / Notes:

"Strong women don't play the victim. Don't make themselves look pitiful and don't point fingers. They stand and they deal." – Mandy Hale

Date:

Daily Habits To Build

- [ ] Stayed Hydrated
- [ ] 30 Minutes Exercise
- [ ] 1 Junk Food Avoided
- [ ] Get Up 1 Hour Early
- [ ]

Intention For The Day:

Goal/Who I Want to Be:

10 Things I Am Grateful For Today / Notes:

"It's your job to show up for your own life and fight for your own dreams." – Rachel Hollis

Date:

Daily Habits To Build

- ☐ Stayed Hydrated
- ☐ 30 Minutes Exercise
- ☐ 1 Junk Food Avoided
- ☐ Get Up 1 Hour Early
- ☐

Intention For The Day:

Goal/Who I Want to Be:

10 Things I Am Grateful For Today / Notes:

"Life shrinks or expands in proportion to one's courage." – Anais Nin

Date:

Daily Habits To Build

- [ ] Stayed Hydrated
- [ ] 30 Minutes Exercise
- [ ] 1 Junk Food Avoided
- [ ] Get Up 1 Hour Early
- [ ]

Intention For The Day:

Goal/Who I Want to Be:

10 Things I Am Grateful For Today / Notes:

"Nothing is wasted. Every single moment is preparing you for the next." – Rachel Hollis

Date:

Daily Habits To Build

- ☐ Stayed Hydrated
- ☐ 30 Minutes Exercise
- ☐ 1 Junk Food Avoided
- ☐ Get Up 1 Hour Early
- ☐

Intention For The Day:

Goal/Who I Want to Be:

10 Things I Am Grateful For Today / Notes:

"Doubt is a killer. You just have to know who you are and what you stand for." – Jennifer Lopez

Date:

Daily Habits To Build

- [ ] Stayed Hydrated
- [ ] 30 Minutes Exercise
- [ ] 1 Junk Food Avoided
- [ ] Get Up 1 Hour Early
- [ ]

Intention For The Day:

Goal/Who I Want to Be:

10 Things I Am Grateful For Today / Notes:

"Someone else doesn't get to tell you who you can be." – Rachel Hollis

Date:

Daily Habits To Build

- [ ] Stayed Hydrated
- [ ] 30 Minutes Exercise
- [ ] 1 Junk Food Avoided
- [ ] Get Up 1 Hour Early
- [ ]

Intention For The Day:

Goal/Who I Want to Be:

10 Things I Am Grateful For Today / Notes:

"You have to have confidence in your ability, and then be tough enough to follow through." – Rosalyn Carter

Date:

Daily Habits To Build

- [ ] Stayed Hydrated
- [ ] 30 Minutes Exercise
- [ ] 1 Junk Food Avoided
- [ ] Get Up 1 Hour Early
- [ ]

Intention For The Day:

Goal/Who I Want to Be:

10 Things I Am Grateful For Today / Notes:

"Do it in celebration of your ability to do so, regardless of what anyone else thinks." – Rachel Hollis

Thank you.

I want to thank you for purchasing this journal. I hope you've enjoyed completing it as much as I've enjoyed writing it and it helps you on your path toward your goal and your dream.

You can stay in touch with me at my website: https://bjrichardsauthor.com

Or on my Facebook page: https://www.facebook.com/BJ.Richards.Author/

And be sure to check out the other books I've written. You can see some of them on the Recommended Reading pages I've included here, or at my website.

Good luck on your journey to a happier, healthier you!

BONUS! FREE INSPIRATIONAL COLORING BOOK!

Get Yours Here: https://bjrichardsauthor.com/sccb-gsa-jn

Recommended Book

I'm sure you already have this, but just in case, it is strongly recommended you purchase the original work by Ms. Hollis this journal is designed to compliment.

Girl, Stop Apologizing: A Shame-Free Plan for Embracing and Achieving Your Goals by Rachel Hollis

You can purchase it here: https://www.amazon.com/Girl-Stop-Apologizing-Shame-Free-Embracing-ebook/dp/B07DT7VJ8T

Recommended: Get The Whole Set

The Perfect Workbook for This Program:

Many readers find it helpful to use a workbook to help them implement lessons and go deeper into the material that is presented.

I've created a workbook that is the perfect companion to the original work by Ms. Hollis, *Girl Stop Apologizing*. In my workbook you'll find worksheets and exercises designed to draw in your own life experiences so you can capitalize on what Ms. Hollis is presenting.

I think you'll love it!

Workbook Companion for Girl Stop Apologizing by Rachel Hollis: A Shame-Free Plan for Embracing and Achieving Your Goals by BJ Richards

The Perfect Planner for This Program:

You're going to need a place to set up, track and change your schedule on a weekly, monthly and yearly basis.

No problem... I have it covered for you! **My planner is designed specifically for the program presented by Ms. Hollis** in her original work, *Girl Stop Apologizing*. This will help you make your journey even easier!

Planner for Girl Stop Apologizing by Rachel Hollis: A Shame-Free Plan for Embracing and Achieving Your Goals by BJ Richards

You may also be interested in some of my other books:

1) Find out what coconut oil can really do for you without all the hype. Check out my best-selling book: *Coconut Oil Breakthrough: Boost Your Brain, Burn the Fat, Build Your Hair* by BJ Richards

Check it out here: https://www.amazon.com/Coconut-Oil-Breakthrough-Boost-Brain-ebook/dp/B01EGBA1FW/

2) Do you have a dog? Here's another best seller you may be interested in. You'll find out to deal with a number of issues safely and inexpensively at home. Find out all about it in my best-seller: *Coconut Oil and My Dog: Natural Pet Health for My Canine Friend* by BJ Richards

You can check it out here: https://www.amazon.com/Coconut-Oil-My-Dog-Natural-ebook/dp/B01MUF93U1/

3) Did you know apple cider vinegar and baking soda have some amazing health benefits? Plus, you can use them for so many things in the home and save a ton of money.

You'll find out all about it my boxset: *Apple Cider Vinegar and Baking Soda 101 for Beginners Box Set* by BJ Richards

Check it out here: https://www.amazon.com/Apple-Cider-Vinegar-Baking-Beginners-ebook/dp/B07DPCLWGB/

You can also go **my website** to find even more books I've written and some recommended by other authors: https://bjrichardsauthor.com

Made in United States
Cleveland, OH
06 June 2025